The Confessions of a Poet

The Confessions Series

BY: ERIC GOODNIGHT
ART: KENNEDY CONNER

THE CONFESSIONS OF A POET

The Confessions Series

BY: ERIC GOODNIGHT

ART: KENNEDY CONNER

Published and Produced by ART the TOUR™; Partner of Make It Poetry LLC
2013

First Printing: 2013

ISBN 978-1-304-64820-4

ART the TOUR™:Make It Poetry LLC
Fishers, IN 46037
Fishers, Indiana 46037

www.artthetour.com

Influence

"Is it so bad, then, to be misunderstood? Pythagoras was misunderstood, and Socrates, and Jesus, and Luther, and Copernicus, and Galileo, and Newton, and every pure and wise spirit that ever took flesh. To be great is to be misunderstood."

— Ralph Waldo Emerson, Self Reliance

"Keep away from people who try to belittle your ambitions. Small people always do that, but the really great make you feel that you, too, can become great."
— Mark Twain

"Let your influence be great, that it'd be good and not evil. Love and seek the truth. For the influence truth, will be as well the influence of you. That it is for all you do."

—Eric Goodnight

Contents

Acknowledgements

I would like to thank my teachers whom would be everyone in which I have had the pleasure of knowing, My Cover Artist, Supporters of The Confessions Series, my Sponsors who have supported the whole process Gallery 116 and Academy of Dance Arts and my family without whose help this book would never have been completed.

Thank you for your support and patience.

THIS IS IT!!!

Introduction

I feel it to be a duty to live life for Love and express freely your emotions. That from expression truth may influence the least emotionally and mentally aware. Those with weak minds and strong hearts. I have lived with addiction. I have denied everyone I love this inevitable truth in ignorance. Including myself. Drawing me further into the thieving dependency that was my addiction to a high. I have lived and still live with the fear of temptation, tomorrow, and the worst evil the failures and trials of my loved ones.

I found in this life that truth is harder to come by than it would be to find a million dollars. I know now that everyone must express themselves personably. I am pleased with this truth. You must be your selves. For, something that isn't where it belongs will surely stick out, a screw that doesn't fit will fall out, and a boat with a whole will sink. So, be yourself and Express yourself because the truth oh, even the suppressed truth will manifest. It is best to let your heart which is passionately and honestly bias to truth guide

your tongue than your mind which calculates with irrational lies a preferred outcome. Which, in time will have failed you.

That brings me to the Truth of Adventure. You decide what is beneficial. For me it was not sports, superficial work, or money, yet words and truth that gives me satisfaction. So, I chose to write and express my truth with poetry.

I am a seeker of this, the truth.

Dead, Diseased, Relieved, Insane... With reason being the sanity of my following. My understanding the world, I'm alone with one voice to mind. Listening to the world in my head as it is the world I live.

Dead, to a world that hides truth in lies, hoping to gain what should never be theirs, taking what others have lost. To empty a coffin where rest an idea. While lies a soul belief, silenced because the truth in a world where lies rein true is cause lost in the chaos, of misunderstanding, lost reason, misfortune, and pain. The lies that are true, true because it's a lie. Which in this life the cleverest lies are true, but the simple truth isn't...?

Diseased, the diagnosis.. Human nature, in which instinct is lost with ability to truly care or hold compassion or passion in our hands just as we would wield a weapon. Plagued by post-traumatic stress in which symptoms of regret, anxiety, and delusion, in which instinct is portrayed. Drawn in a permanent ink, that bled on life a canvas on which the permanence of a misguided past that begs hurt on a mind. Gives life to what humanity killed. So, not dead not gone but diseased.

Relieved, of all burdens that are not put where it can be buried. A landfill of waste of an era that loves a thing that can't give back, love of a thought that gives a dream. A thought which is still loved more than the idea of what life gives back, something that loves more than a thought, a thought which I bid a brain. A brain, which knows all but how to love. So, to think of relaxing without effort is an empty blunt, to which to be at peace you must work and give, put in effort, work, idea, to know of a peace at which you can relax. To relax without giving is only to be relieved of crisis, which without knowing crisis one cannot know how to relax.

Insane, to think that one can be cured of the lies that burn true. Sick with lack of compassion, and robbed of an idea, the idea that love is one's ability to give all they've got to their beliefs and life's fortunes. Buried by its lies in the chaos of a true lie. Without a fair trial, pain is as real in a seed as is the tree for a tree knows of pain from falling from a height, life, life catches you when you fall. Ripped from an idea and shot down with thoughts, a number, a heart, an idea, a home, a life is a dream that can't be chased or even dreamed just real. Crazy its wrong, jaded, very naive.. Life and understanding is a man's truth and justification of age. A man's ability to know love, and life, for what it is.

Misty green disguise

Like gravity I'm pulled into your eyes
Your eyes which brings my emotions life
The light of my past life.
Trapped I see only you, your eyes...
You I know, but there's something
That hides. A girl for some reason lost it seems.
Yet my surprise when you find me.
I see past your misty green disguise.
For your eyes tell me what you see.

Life of Word

Speak, write, hum, laugh, and think.
For, a single word expressed,
is a breath that gives life..
Poetry.

For, the Good of the World

For, the good of the world.
When, I am graced with life as my age.
I hope to live freely, escaping life's mal-illusions of control
To love purely & sin nothing
To speak lightly, for my nature shall be gentle yet brusque, assertively blunt!
Time the vault that harbors memories, will hold from me none of my triumphs and success but only my cruel beginnings.
I will have learned.
"There's a calling in all of us"
It can't be found, only embraced for, it was never lost.
And be satisfied with watching life on earth unfold from my front porch for I shared the good of my heart with my neighbors.
For, all the good in the world we are a part of.

Bring Me Peace

Mind, like a ship wreck sinking taking
passengers with the ship.
Me alone because I drew my own boat from a
shaky shore.
At night, in dark, alone I am
Freezing cold.
a sea now, ice traps me alone in an everlasting
wreck.
This burning regret and grief slowly edging a
meltdown freeing me to the sea.
Gods waters of wrath, begins to wrap around
me
Trapped in my mind a wreck absent to the rest
of the world
I hold a hope in the manifestation of this fate
but alone I yell out to only one name
"God!"
I ask without fear, only in sadness.
Bring from me this grief.

I hope for mercy.
I always plead for love.
But Oh lord bring me peace.
Glory to you lord, for from my
Wreck I am now free

Love

More, less than yesterday, today I am overwhelmed.

Patient, but ready for the endeavors to build you a home in the oasis of my heart.

Lonely to myself without you, I rest my thoughts.

The ideas, the truth. The truth of these ideas, are yet so invincible and completely bulletproof. The idea that I love you more than my soul is mine.

The idea that like a shadow, Love.. Our Love is a visual and an illusion to be completely real that of the light and solidity it creates something that takes the shape of what lies in front of it.

and is again completely bullet proof and is as lasting as day and night which both the sun and moon know, a timeless and forever partnership, and forever union. LOVE

The art of word. One word, one story

A picture I'm told, is worth a thousand words. I say tragedy is that untold story. For, a word alone in my experience paints a picture.

To Find Love

Blue skies, when sunny dies. I wonder where were you. Time flies when April skies turn a deeper blue. that's the time when you and I should talk a talk till the clock strikes one or two...then lay in bed and cuddle until sleep can cover you. Nighty, night we close our eyes until we meet again. hen eyes of two that's me and you open to see again, a friend. or more. to that we'll do the same again

Stuck...

To compare a wound or illness that leaves us bed ridden...
To the lies that live around us
Framed by the ignorance of our actions
Our innocence lost, our intentions maimed
No longer free, the walls of emotion masoned' by the guilt of your heart.
widens but every wall being stronger than the last, you.
you, are stuck. brittle the heart, you use Anger as a shield.
Running from everything that is Love.
Your ambitions still, yet alive.
your heart mortared you bricks of agony with strange yet common Self-pity.
you lose your sight of Dreams.
Or at the least the ones that were the honest you.
You the Broken one sees the truth of evil. A Simple pleasure. A meal in a capsule.
Scared, you feel your hopelessness grow holding you back from that which is your true destiny

And your worst mistake is you forget to look up.
Until The war in yourself tires and your mind surrenders to your Heart and your heart to the truths of self-worth.
Pride left on the battle grounds Love is again bound to wealth of your future.
Truth is Now more than ever a Virtue
So, is there a truth that will now set us free?
Assume you are too, stuck..
Now, ask yourself why and how, for the truth.

To Choose, How?

Love, Life, Hate, or Death
So many choices
Hate begs Mortality
Mortality instigates Dark feelings
To live with yourself..., How?
Death is Evil.
Hate is Evil.
Now, how many choices?
Love desires Life
Life knows and seduces Light, to Love
unconditionally everyone..., How?
How, difficult then..
Will it be to hate?
How, difficult is it to choose Love?
How, difficult is it to choose Life?
For Love is Good...
Evil deceives you to dread the vulnerability that
is Love. Fear.
For, fear of the death of this love causes fatal
envy, to hate, to kill.. to die.

Yet, Love tells the truth fear hides from the newly passionate.
Have you made your choice?
So, it is expected that you choose.. but How?
Trust.. to choose, how you love.

The Plea

To my Persecutor,
I am guilty, blame the crime
Convictions, I have made scarce in light of those public
Overshadowed are my wrongs, when someone leads me wrong.
That begs the question.
Guilty or not Guilty?
The personal witness of the witnessed.. Me. Builds bias, yet learns conviction of self in self.
In that I meet my persecutor.
Subtle lies, true lies.
Innocent, But How?
Because the followers aren't the guilty, just got caught right? No!
Lies... Now, the Truth.
Guilty/No Excuses.. Just Understanding.
I look now in this light acknowledging my mistakes.
Insane attempts at growing up, corrupt guidance, self-influenced grief.
To not admit guilt in any light would prove ignorant.

To say just the same, I am not Human
Instead, I understand myself and the community of peers in which I've invited to influence me
Success! Only this one most valuable, for i have learned... Thank You.
I ask you now for understanding, The Plea.. Life lesson learned
And you.. You ask, how I plead..
GUILTY.

3 Of A Kind

Standing here alone watching lights
running by
I see so many things
In front of this building
I see so many things
There's three lights spotting me
2 out here standing behind me
and I that watches me through the window
pane
They share with we three likenesses of myself
One just in front of me that stands as I do
but meeting back where I stand
Without a doubt, these are mine
Shadows standing outside
Meet my 3 of a Kind

Smoke Aside

Foolishness,
Failure you can't beat.
The trickery is the undefeated.
Smoke that is breathed yet cannot breathe.
Death, takes life.
Understand this irony.
For, when will the clouds get too thick?
When, will you clear the smoke aside
Smoke Aside
This homicide/suicide
It seems that to put Smoke Aside is suicide.
So, who's the killer in this homicide?
There is life aside, the terminally congested.
Conquer and expose this illusion
Defeat the success of failure and finally put
your smoke aside.

I Love You, I Love You Not

This flower holds countless petals.
Just the same I have countless reasons why I love and countless more of why I shouldn't.
I love you.., I love you not.. This flower almost empty now, we have destroyed.
Yet, finally as the last petal is ripped from the once beautifully full flower to lay a-top the rest in the pile..
I love you!..
Though, I now realize without reason. Only now this flower, destroyed lays without reason lifeless..
What have we done?

Better For You

Bricks chiseled in sorrow
At the expense of my heart
I build this wall at a speed which doesn't allow
for question
Fast and in short time
Short and sweet, you are
Just the same are my words
At least, this time.
Now, time my heart desires but time my heart
requires you know?
Yet, an eternity has no time
Love too has no time to bear

SO, UNDERSTAND ME NOW.

How long will I Love you?
What will be of an eternity?
And in the same.
What will be of an eternity knowing now, for
now, or forever I'll be without you?
Will we have a chance in our eternal years?
For love.
I must journey for the answer.
Yet again and now forever, God's Grace is
Among You and I.
So, if Love has no watch.
How long is eternity?

JUST UNDERSTAND.

I have to be directed by the Lord and his
winds.
Learn and Teach
Love and Preach.
Justice won't come from impairing thoughts
Should have, would have, could have.
Just the demands of truth.
I will, in practice.
I am, in faith.
.....Better.
And should, could and would be better for you if
that's what you want.
But, for now understand that even at my best I
could, should, and would be better for you.

FAREWELL SOLDIER

Farewell Soldier.
Those words I hoped I never get to say.
Be safe and think of me here.
I work today because of you, my siblings play because of you, my family and church sings because of you, I am free to be an me because of you, my life is well because of you, school I love because of you, life I have because of you.
I pray every day for you, for I've learned to pray every moment because of you. Gratitude has made me fearless I can make many mistakes but because of you, fear shall never be one.
I now fear less, and run to fight the battle you can't. So you too fear less. You fight a battle so tragic one can only fear. But fear less.. one less fear. It's just as easy as the words trust and believe, because you are the strong one.
God is stronger than your enemy even when you're not.

Though, you just have to let him be. So let him.
Thank you soldier for I would have never
learned. So make no mistakes. Fear Less.
Now, for you because of you I embrace the once
dreaded words..
Farewell Soldier, until we meet again.

Safe is to have passion...but anger..

Live to have life
hold life as the closest of enemies
and death your closest of friends
destined to fail
only once to tell
fear abuses the mind
pain fire god life
death to what is absently
watching your every move
only to spoil in your failure
capture at once
only to release
and once again

Renew
or to the devils comfort(safe?)
his way he'll have (anger!)
to you an enemy you call friend
to fear God, the one you can only depend
to believe is to hold comfort with fear
to hold comfort is to have passion and will
passion to which rest in life
to hold passion is to live
live to have life.

Beautiful Disguise

So, Beautiful
Your soul is Gorgeous
Oh, Beautiful
Everything about you I adore
Does one forget a Rose?
Then how could one forget you?
I love the smile your face holds
Picture Perfect.. your face, beautifully
framed by your hair.
Your eyes mesmerizes me
Memories of you put me in a trance.
So, Beautiful
I'm addicted to your body.
Smoking Hot
How I miss the sensual kisses
The caress of your Goddess like frame
against mine.
You are God sent. The Angel I pray saves
me.

But, oh Beautiful

What a disguise.. Why hide in your
insecurities, your beauty?
When you hide in my presence your girly
anxiety.
I know I'm missed.
missing you I hide in the same disguise
The air we share seems a lot fresher
So, lose the disguise. Tell me your heart.
Thoughts of the mind are flawed.
Desires of the heart are flawless.
I love you. So tell me you do.
Do what you verb.
Love what you love.
When well you return?
When will I meet you again?
Your quite Beautifully Disguised.
From me, you can run.
From me, you can hide.
Yet, I will always see through your
Beautiful Disguise.

Eye for, An I

This is the time.. 9 reasons: 3 truths 6 plus 4 sunsets since Cupid's day. Tears bathe my eyes with no regard and intent for movement. And yet I see in 20/13. This vision so clear is my being and future. It seems the one whom with I've prayed, can see 13 months forward but I can see the mile. 20 years she wanted to rewind before it began only when irate. I pray to never anger her again. Loving jezebel has been tough rewarding and has failed me I loved the most I could even when I begged fondness to be enough. Now, as I age. I speak my future 2014, 2015, 2016, 2017, 2018, 2019, 2020. 20/20. I feel wasted, for as I age I fear I'll lose my sight just the same. Vision lost I see 20 months to be a future and in frustration wish them to pass. Love, it'd be that would change me. So, oh young visionary don't waste your Eye for an I love you is hard to find.

WITH YOUR PURCHASE OF THE PREQUEL OF THE CONFESSIONS OF A POET THE NOVEL. YOUR INVITED TO THE STORY ORIGINAL CONFESSIONS OF A POET AS THE ONE OF 35 to PURCHASE OUR BOOK.

(ORIGINAL CERTIFICATE THAT WILL BE GOOD FOR YOUR NEXT PURCHASE WITH ART THE TOUR™. FOR, FREE MERCHANDISE OF $35 OR LESS VALUE. FROM, OUR IMPENDING STORE SELECTION. AVAILABLE FROM OUR SPONSOR GALLERY 116 OR RECEIVE THE FULL STORY VERSION OF "THE CONFESSIONS OF A POET")

1st and Original copy sold. FREE Merchandise
ART the TOUR™

Visit us,
ART the TOUR's Artist and The Author of the Confessions
artthetour.com
facebook.com/ARTisOURs

Sneak peak of the Drama of the Up and Coming Novel-Poem "Novel-try" By the Author.

TRUTH VS. SOCIALITIES

Sleep is something i do well, because of the honest truth i tell.. But for you it's hard to take, so out of sleep you wake. toss and turning side to side because you know that i don't lie. so a liar out of me you make because the simple truth you can't take.. so another truth I've yet to tell is lying gets you only a trip to hell. Oh and i did write a book wait.. two. but bragging i don't do. but whether you believe me is up to you. After the following I'll be done. again the truth...this is no fun. creative but i run. always down for having fun. me i hold no gun just words that say yet again the truth may be life's only true friend. jealous is never much you know just as well, remember lunch? and who was thereafter to help you out because there that day i was no doubt. and Atlanta Georgia where i resign, here my true friends never lie. [by this point the people i intended this for are going to stop reading] Lie(you):"i lied about everything to everyone in PORTAGE about MY LIFE!!" (Truth i still told.) but the only real lie about a person's life is told by fake people that doesn't know. Portage had to draw a map to be on a map. If you ask me that's fake. just as true as fat kids love cake. Truth(I):"I can say that i honestly you and your people are fake, that i tried to be a friend, lies I've never been, but hurt i am the most so to those who waste their time hating me for false reasons do to my honest tongue together you fake people belong.. and if I'm the one you hate most, forgive but forget or a ghost to you better yet"

Georgia's real, Atlanta, you, ha my city's much bigger too!

I like Portage don't get wrong. but as for the people.. the truth and them don't get along. but a selected few i trust, because the truth to them is a must. (Casey Timmons, Faith Jeremiah, Zack and Nick Penn, Kevin English, Simone, Big John, Marlon, Dennis, Emily, Katie (music chic), Rachel (ginger), Jake Moran(ginger snap), Morgan, Chantal, Tyler Johnson, taco, and Marita) and there's a few more but don't assume... that i.."forgot a name", "or left you out on accident". but i admit there's maybe 3..no.. maybe four more. it doesn't matter but to the few i commend. Just know you'll always have a friend. As for all the rest, all i wish for you is the best.

P.S. This is geared toward those with anything at all against me. not to harm, but to say this yet again very friendly. Simply.. F.U! I mean your Freaking Unbelievable..

TRUTH: Eric Devaule Goodnight Jr. is my name.

More about the Author

Born in Battle Creek, MI a JR to an absent a father.. My sperm donor.. A man Daniel Taylor III came into the lives of my four siblings and mother with three children of his own. I'm a Christian but only speak words that are familiar to all, yet only to the intrigue of my beliefs. My mother DeAngela Taylor a Poet herself mesmerized me in a dream of pure verbal bliss. Words, a charm of Goodness and relief, strength and understanding.. Pure Love. And truth this is why I write. To right/write the wrongs of a misguided past and to share in the grace in which one is blessed, and ever so grateful. Fear no death. Not even of ink and embrace experience. My poems are my confessions. I am a hopeful poet. I have a great love for the art of this "Life". ART is in everything, words only witness to this. I am Eric Goodnight and this is my story . All my poetry is me. Yet, I know who you are. For it is who I am after all we're all human. Receive my words only as the voice of a humbled, boy transitioned into a humble man.

www.ingramcontent.com/pod-product-compliance
Ingram Content Group UK Ltd.
Pitfield, Milton Keynes, MK11 3LW, UK
UKHW020217250726
13967UKWH00001B/48

9 781304 648204